D1605757

About AMONG THE ENIGMAS

Robert Murphy knows what an imposter you are. He knows about your endless negotiations with the universe. He knows you are bluffing and how desperately you struggle with the terror of being found out. He's not blowing the whistle, mind you—but he is going to make sure that you're in on the joke that you're making of yourself. Murphy's is a voice, though, that can pull off this trick. Even in the midst of exorcising (exercising?) demons—which he quite literally does—there is a kindness, warmth and a wit that so many poets hope they will grow into but never do. *Among the Enigmas* is a lovely, authentic book and just what you need after another long day of faking it, "As if it were a secret vice to be a deceiver/indistinguishable from the one deceived."

—GEOFFREY WOOLF
author of *Lrarn to Love Explosives*

In *Among the Enigmas*, his finest collection thus far, Murphy has the courage not to impose himself on the language but to allow it to speak plainly from a deep well of feeling and conviction. Rhythm and rhyme mark his discoveries and render them at once luminous and concrete. These are real poems, poems that confront universal enigmas but nevertheless speak to us with a singularity and eloquence of their own. In his marvelous "Imp" poems, Murphy writes:

Who are we, anyway, to be so ill conceived?
I say it's you, you say it's me.
As if it were a secret vice to be a deceiver
Indistinguishable from the one deceived.

—HENRY WEINFIELD
author of *Without Mythologies*

Robert Murphy's jocular seriousness is on full display in *Among the Enigmas*. Even when he's paying tribute to his hero William Bronk in the opening section, he can't resist the urge to puncture clichés: "No glass, no empty, no full." Moving through the familiar landscape of religious, primarily Christian, iconography, Murphy re-imagines the story of Lazarus as the desire for oblivion—"NO!" and "DON'T", and/ "WHO DO YOU THINK YOU ARE?" For Murphy, dreams are our "true familiars," the ones who would prefer to turn us "inside out." The ancient, unreconstructed, power of interiority, the source of vatic poetry, is Murphy's true god, not the cold comfort of "The body lifeless. The body born again." Always retreating to his family of enigmas, Robert Murphy is not going quietly "To the brink, the cliff edge/…to slaughter."

—TYRONE WILLIAMS
author of *Black Brigade, Adventures of Pi* and other books

Like other poets I know who admire Robert Murphy, when I read him, I think of Shakespeare. I don't think the comparison too much of a stretch because this comes from his lifetime of reading; from his desire for words, lines and stanzas to make music; and from his understanding that humans aren't cleanly divided into good and evil, innocent and guilty. Murphy speaks to moral complexity, and does so playfully, subverting clichés and laying out mysteries. *Among the Enigmas* presents witch trials that could be taking place in the present moment; the sleeping princess whose consent we've always taken for granted; the cow whose story-end is taken for granted, too; a modern Puck (Imp), perpetually dissatisfied; and flowers that, surviving the man who planted them, are "never to be in the same way seen."

—DEBORAH DIEMONT

To spend time with Robert Murphy's *Among the Enigmas* is to be in the presence of a great soul. At the center of Murphy's vision — for he is, make no mistake, a visionary poet in the line of Blake, in touch with truths that exist far beyond the page — is a battle between stasis and dynamism, between appearance and reality, between Truth and a diversity of truths. In his stunningly bleak psalm, "As if Cattle," Murphy observes the herd in "bland, bowed calm" as long as its "hunger, thirst, or fear" is slaked, — that is, until it meets its mortal fate. "Jumping Jehoshaphat!" he exclaims in "The Appearance of it All," one of the volume's finest poems, "Only a Holy Fool/Would come down here" to attempt to reason with common sense and the world of appearances. While Murphy's poems are animated by a dynamic spirit, they're thoroughly skeptical of received truths. That skepticism breeds a black humor and a wild, Joycean paronomasia. The punning bursts forth in Murphy's major sequence of nine "Imp" poems, which *imp*ortunately explore, in the persona of a Socratic inchling/inkling, various *imp*onderables, *imp*ositions, *imp*ostures, and a great deal more. Adding to the serious fun is the engrossing artwork of Donald Golder, which engages with, rather than illustrates, Murphy's verse.

—DAVID M. KATZ
author, *Stanzas on Oz* and *Claims of Home*

For Jeff, May He continue His Song
Long Among The Enigmas

Blessings & More

[signature]

2/9/20

A Prolegomenon

At the outset of his volume, *Among the Enigmas*, Robert Murphy tells us he had sent the late poet William Bronk "the poet's flower, *poeticus narcissus* . . . an echo of the Mediterranean world/ from which they come, pure white, with six (as it is described/ in the catalogs) perianth segments on a single stem." True to his word, Murphy delivers to us poetry as pure as Bronk's own stripped down language. Without resorting to metaphor or other rhetorical embellishments, the clean lines of his verse engage with existential issues in plain statements appropriate to human perception. The result washes his subjects clean of their historical conditionals. He gives Being-as-such the freedom to create whatever fiction it chooses to inhabit. Tangled in the elements of the natural world as well as in the set of words we are handed down, the poet's subjects seek to understand themselves in terms of the universe in which they live and which lives in them. That this world is stripped of its societal niceties and ideological facades allows for many powerful moments in Murphy's work. The book's last section, Imp, particularly highlights the resulting struggles. With deadpan wit reminiscent of Berryman's Henry, Imp wrestles with self and asks at one point, "who are we, anyway, to be so ill conceived?" But the answer has already been suggested. While the volume is haunted by Bronk, these masterful poems definitely belong to Robert Murphy, who notes, "fall and fall and fall/ the son, after long practice/ become father of himself after all."

The poems here are paired with many wonderful works by the visual artist Donald Golder. The mostly ink and watercolor images seem to occupy a subliminal space somewhere between fairytale illustration and the surrealism of

Max Ernst. Line drawings with startling juxtapositions, thin washes of color corresponding to fields rather than objects, and heavily textured works in which foreground and background merge create a visual lexicon easily recognizable and profoundly uncanny. The dream world they describe sets a tone appropriate to Murphy's work and the two enhance each other in this beautiful volume.

Together, Murphy and Golder's collaboration allows the reader of *Among the Enigmas* to transgress the porous borders between the living and the dead, between landscape and interiority, and finally between Self and Other. Somehow, we learn in due course, "We are who we say we are."

—STEVEN WINHUSEN

Author, *Blue Chip City Book of the Dead*

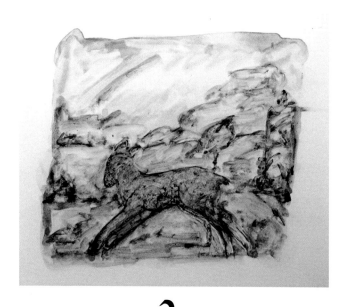

Among the Enigmas

poems by

ROBERT MURPHY

artwork by

DONALD GOLDER

DOS MADRES

2019

DOS MADRES PRESS INC.
P.O.Box 294, Loveland, Ohio 45140
www.dosmadres.com   editor@dosmadres.com

Dos Madres is dedicated to the belief that the small press is essential to the vitality of contemporary literature as a carrier of the new voice, as well as the older, sometimes forgotten voices of the past. And in an ever more virtual world, to the creation of fine books pleasing to the eye and hand.

Dos Madres is named in honor of Vera Murphy and Libbie Hughes, the "Dos Madres" whose contributions have made this press possible.

Dos Madres Press, Inc. is an Ohio Not For Profit Corporation and a 501 (c) (3) qualified public charity. Contributions are tax deductible.

Executive Editor: Robert J. Murphy

Illustration & Book Design: Elizabeth H. Murphy
www.illusionstudios.net

Typeset in Adobe Garamond Pro & Herman Decanus AH
ISBN 978-1-948017-52-7
Library of Congress Control Number: 2019944631

ACKNOWLEDGEMENTS

"Imp," "Imp Goes Fishing Anyway," "Imp as Imponderable," "Impetigo," and "An Imposition" appeared in *From Behind the Blind* (Dos Madres Press 2013).

"The Bottom Line" appeared in *The Marsh Hawk Review* (Fall 2016) and *Beans and Rice* (June 2016).

"Where the Unborn are Concerned" and "Shelter in Place appeared in *Galatea Resurrects* (December 2016).

"Fellow Travelers" appeared in *Live Mag!* (Issue 15, 2018).

"The Last Oracle," in slightly different form, appeared in *Prints into Poetry* (Gravity Free Press 2018).

For Donald and Elizabeth who have given Body to what otherwise would have neither face, nor hand, nor eye — without a leg to stand on.

TABLE of contents

Imp

Index of Art

Not much left of the creature to say it was
. . . bones scattered . . .
could have been, except for the many sharp teeth
along the jawline, the bones of a child:
The bones of a child buried in a man,
buried in the nature of the world.

Foreword
Afterword

The Lay Of The Land – Hudson Falls New York, *Just This Side of Elysium*

That it could be at all difficult to say exactly how
Bronk's blue squill, *scilla siberica* survived
the frozen Parian of his winters there,
when we should know by its name to have faith
in such that bears the season of return.

It is, of course, our own return we doubt – not theirs.

I sent Bill the poet's flower, *poeticus narcissus*, variety
old pheasant eye. Those ones that are fragrant,
almost impossibly so, an echo of the Mediterranean world
from which they come, pure white, with six (as it is described
in the catalogs) perianth segments on a single stem,
petals slightly recurved; with a small, red rimmed
ruffled yellow cup into which you might pour yourself
to lie within reflected – the last of its kind to bloom,
                                        late spring.

The zodiacal twelve were planted where he could watch them
grow from his kitchen window. Someone else's window now
no matter how they look, never to be in the same way seen.

I've brought one into the house to show you.
It's in a vase on the sill by the cellar door
just this side of Elysium,
closed up, furled, if not quite folded like a letter
still in its envelope waiting to be read –
stamped: not with *Return to sender*, but with
From a place no longer able to be received.

2

3

The Last Oracle

Might be that old man
dunk'n his false teeth in his morning coffee,
one more sleepless three AM,
the only customer in the joint,
and I there to his life apprenticed.
Washing dishes at Apollo's,
the all-night Greek diner
>*you know where it is,*
>   *I don't have to tell you*
stone-deaf as he was, and waxing,
as he often did, philosophic . . .
said he'd, anyway, seen it all before,
and didn't need, or want to hear,
a snot-bit more about it.

Among the Enigmas

The Real Problem Is

Whatever life we think we live,
Colonized, inhabited by
Thoughts as much unlived as we
Whose words survive us—
Life having fled with the naming of things
Abandoned in despair of us.

The Times

We see the times as our own
Rather than what every day *is*
Brought back to life in us to live

Where what *was*, otherwise,
Would never think to do, *does*,

And remembered so
Time and Again
Has its way with us.

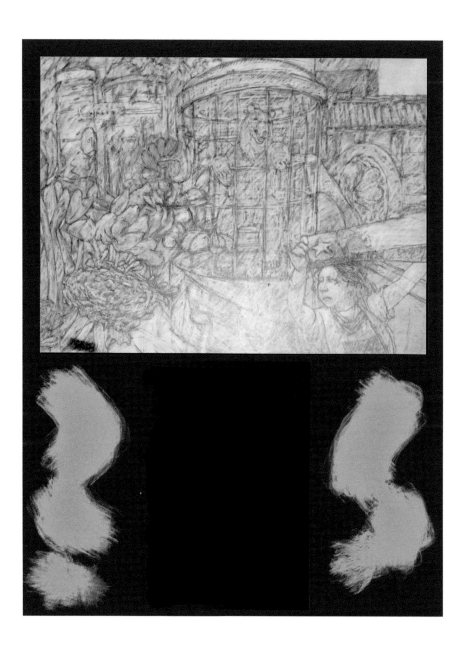

Take a long hard look in the mirror,
        Can't you hear what you are saying?

Nothing harder to look upon than when
The sea, the sky, and the horizon are one.

Put your ear to it. I mean really put your ear to it.
Not one word, not one word . . .

Look here, for God's sake,
Dare you . . . call it your own.

13

Father of Himself after All

O, the need to rise.
And in the rising fall,
And fall and fall and fall,
The son, after long practice,
Become father of himself after all.

To awaken between light and night
In the marriage bed, the placental bed,
Bed of the dead of the ghosts we are
Each morning found in body wed
To a dream of the world newly born.

Whose Voices

What did he want to hear,
As much as he could bear?
Not the excuses.
Not the reasoned
Why of it, but
What was always
True to its word.

Out of the starlight,
Out of the stardust
Of its enfoldments:
Not the keening dead—
Not these ghosts
Locked in the unutterable . . .
Voices busy in his head.

Those in control of what you think you know,
    Know your favorite watering hole.

It's not that the glass is half empty
Or rather that the glass is half full,

But the surprise at hand
In the thought of it there . . .

No glass, no empty, no full.

The Age of Consent

It's about seduction, or maybe it's
More like that Sleeping Beauty kiss,
The Prince in still-frame frozen.
Poised above Snow White's ruby lips . . .
She, as she has always been,
Perfectly chaste, almost,
But not quite yet, a Princess.

O, it's all about breathing life
Back into life, . . . isn't it?

And so what happens next?

No offense. And call it what you will:
Diminished capacity,
Under the influence . . .

Or both.

Anyway, it's Lazarus you'll be wanting
To talk to here, not me.
"NO!" and "DON'T", and
"WHO DO YOU THINK YOU ARE?"
Wasn't an option for him either.

The Appearance of It All

Among the appearances,
Where common sense prevails.
Hidden in plain sight as they always are
Right under our noses . . .
(if not the coffee, try the roses)
And just out of earshot too.
   – "Listen up!" –
Fact is, if facts mattered,
And they don't.
Not in any real world:
Priest, Rabbi, Mullah,
Good Time Evangelical Rock and Roller.
Dear Mother of God, it's true.
And you're dead right.
When not for the first time
You find a serpent
In your shoe . . .

"Jumping Jehoshaphat!"

My friend, have faith.
Experience tells us,
Only a Holy Fool
Would come down here
As you do now,
To reason with it.

The Practice

That we have names
For everything under the sun.
Whole books full and quite a few others
On the tip of the tongue . . .

At least as many as those angels
Reportedly at dance on the head of a pin.
And not one word of them
With a leg to stand on.

. . . .

Search for it under a bushel.
Search for it under a rock.
So much falls on deaf ears,
As if they actually could.

At the Border

We come bearing false identities—
Trying to convince the authorities
We are who we say we are:

Those who know us best.
Ourselves being the ones we are
Most desperate to convince.

23

Last Night? The Night Before? Last Week?

(The Salem Witch Trials: February 1692 - May 1693)

Did you hear it?
How could you not?
Last night? The night before?
Last week?

O, I tell you, I heard it plain as day,
Though it was midnight dark.
And not a sound at all.
A phantom trumpet call.

I stood up straight in bed.
My hair, I tell you, stood on end.
I felt something crawl across my neck
And it was thick as rope.

All the pins had dropped.
The crickets hid their chirp.
A quiet spread so far and wide,
You could hear the walking dead outside.

A locket locked with the key inside.
And True or False it knocked.
As if my heart had stopped.
With Judgment's Yes or No.

A gun without report.
A bell that would not toll.
A morning never come.
A mouth without a tongue.

The stitching all undone.
I dared not move to breathe.
Who would take my plea?
Who believe me now?

That in the gibbet's swing of things,
The dread that lay down over me
Wears the Devil's smile.

The Humane Society

What could it possibly mean?

With our toothy grins. Our lolling red
Wolf-in-grandmother's-clothing tongues.
Our mouths at gnaw on the flesh
Of the body of the world.

Gateway to the endless
Of the unappeasable:
Hell-hole, pie-hole, sewer grate that leads
To its own belly-full of hungers . . .
Unaccountable untold numbers

Of un-lived-lives . . .

Opens wide for its supper,
And for heaven's sake

        sings.

....

When all is lost, In-The-Nick-Of-Time appears
Disguised as The Woodsman sharp of ax—
The Hunter sounding peril's horn,
Come in from out the dark wood
To free us from our selves.

As if Cattle

As if cattle, countless in their bland, bowed calm
Browsed a verdant pasture,
With no more than what borders near
To the ineffable
At stand between *You* and *They*.

And only hunger, thirst, or fear
To otherwise drive them
Beyond what little more than one
Collective sigh might overcome
Trampling their own earthly bonds beneath them.

But feed that hunger, quench the body of its thirst,
Let not the wolf-pack mill about in rumor,
And they will stay
Content within God's image made green acre.
Until it comes, as it always comes,

As if a gate left open in the night,
And they are led,
Not in mad pell-mell or flood,
But like lambs in leisure promenade
To the brink, the cliff edge—

And to slaughter.

Shelter in Place

We have been here
Since the Word came down,
As if from the moment the World began—

We have forgotten so much.

"Shelter in place!"
Not knowing whether
A command, a warning, or a plea—
Come out of the blue,
A voice, in faith, we could not refuse:
"Shelter in place!" we hear and we obey,
"Shelter in place!" Depend on it,
What else is a body to do?
And still we are waiting
To be told what it is at the edge of our lives
That shadows us—
What it is that keeps us so at bay.

"Shelter in place!" Shelter in place!"
Neither knowing how it came to be,
Nor how it must surely end.

We do what we can to pass the time of day.
Some tell stories, others joke,
The more guarded listen and look.
Of the unaccountable, no one will say.
Most try, just as they had before, to work and eat,
Drink in that abide,

And from what store they have
Make love.
In the face of it we do the best we can:
The children unconcernedly play.
Some sleep a bit and dream.
Others think and think on what it all should mean . . .
And not a few, after all is said and done,
Having been so provisioned,

Of how to make it home.

The Bottom Line

I'm sitting at the table where everyone is
Talking at the same time, or trying to,
With their mouths full—
Nobody getting a word in edgewise.
And not a few are smacking their lips,
Even licking them, as dogs do.
So who can be blamed for not being able to hear
The bawling of the cow in the steak tartare,
Or see with startled eyes the prefiguring stain
Emerge from the *boeuf en croute*
Giving face time to the Shroud of Turin.
Or feel the echo of the lamb's last bleat
The moment the hammer comes down,
When there isn't a slitting of throats.
And what with all the wine being served,
Well, you can imagine . . . red as blood . . .
Most here have already forgotten
The dreams they dreamed the night before
Where the potato is both near and far sighted,
Corn has its hearing in the music of the spheres,
And fish their scales beyond weight and measure,
Silent arpeggios with a story to tell about a golden ring,
And not just another fish-tale where the Big One gets away
To pull you hook, line, and sinker into the *salade niçoise* . . .
Your spoon, along with the Flying Dutchman,
At rest on the "bottomless bowl"
Of the *bouilliabaisse*.

God's truth,
It was almost like the wedding at Cana
Where Jesus asks his mother,
What does this have to do with me?
And, I'll admit there was some concern raised
Over the veal cutlet and the *foie gras* . . .
But, Ah, the *côtelettes d'agneau,*
My friend, now those were
A plate-full of Lamb Chops to die for.

Where The Unborn Are Concerned

Difficult enough to be born into any world,
Let alone between piss and shit
And the daily wipe of our bums—
Though that Jesus, that Apuleius knew
The Ass as faithful beast of burden
In the carry of our mortal yearning
Past the postern gate and through
Into every Elysium, Old and New Jerusalem
Where it takes actual work to be a ghost.
Especially when we are told
Over and over, as if we should forget,
It's the thought that counts
That separates us from the herd—
The animal self we both praise and loathe,
"Lived by powers we pretend to understand."
Which is all the more amazing when
We hear from the programmatic
The moment of inception made disease,
Incarnation the beginning of a metastasis,
The unwanted spread of out-of-control-cells,
Leading to another mouth to feed.
The I AM as much as the YOU ARE
Stillborn in the womb—
Never to be returned to the Body
As midwife in the birth of the True—
Or, when it comes to it, gain the Necessary
Error of our ways: no instar to instar
That like stepping-stones appears
As Mohammed's mountain called,

Or as fiery letters, fiery shards,
Out of *the slumbering mass.*
Imagination's appetitions stirred
To neither rise nor fall—
Ashes, embers
Reduced to matters of fact.

If not as You or I,
Who will teach the gods their ABCs?
How will they learn to spell,
Give sentence to, or fully bring to term:
No chance for fate as luck would have it,
But always the right to choose?

Fellow Travelers

You hear them who are unheard,
Oars dipping and rising, dripping
With the watery rhythms of each fey heart.
And almost as if they could be seen
From a distance, eyes fixed on that horizon
To which there is no beyond.
Might be a windup toy mechanical,
Intractable centipede on the move
Across an enormous polished floor.
And pulling as one body against the encompassing
Of that insoluble, unconsolable sea,
Which is as smooth as glass,
And, here, for our purposes, like a mirror
In which the sun appears reflected.
The same sun that looked upon that boy
Carried as far and high
As longing might take him.
And where again and again he rises to his fall.
The rowers slip through the molten sheen
Which quickly freezes behind them as they pass.
A wound that soon as made, closes,
And all in the midst of it frozen fast.
The urge that captains necessity crews,
Unmoved, sails on in silence.
In the spell-bind of their sentence,
Bending to their work; the heat coming off them
As the rank odor of creatures too long penned,
And shoulder to shoulder strain.
The piss and dung of their determined world

They everywhere deny spread beneath their tails.
Reenactment's dead, as the living are when shackled.
At each wrist the mark of time.
Become the ghosts they have to be
In order to survive. As you do now,
And as quickly unknowingly forget,
Paralyzed as in a dream.
The depths from which you struggle to cry out.
Though your dreams, your true familiars
Know you better than they know themselves,
Would whisper into each deaf ear.
Would shake you. Would startle you awake.
Would turn you inside out
To bring you back to life.

for Paul Pines (1941-2018):
fellow dreamer, fellow traveler, . . . Gilgamesh to my Enkidu

The Most by Far

The most by far gainsay it:
That one day The Truth appeared
And spread like a word of mouth contagion.
And that out of The Truth a sword was forged
And placed into the hands of the Righteous.
And the blade had writ upon it Vengeance . . .
For "Vengeance is mine, saith the Lord."
And upon the land a consuming fire was set
That with a rage kills in order to purify:
The Truth that would set us free.
Until no one living, not even those
Among the honored dead in memory,
Would recall who or what it was to be
Before The Truth arrived beguiling:
The hard won, the bitter, the hidden,
And in the search of,
Whole and nothing but The Truth,
"So help me God."
And The Truth was all that mattered.
And we were mad for it.
And everywhere we looked,
Into the very eyes of The Beloved,
Unto the very gaze we give
To the face we face each other with.
All swore it was The Truth . . .
Until The Truth became us:
Its image, if not its very body.

And not a one
Saw in their own likeness
The false witness
Who stood before them.

ZMP

Imp

Lord knows, for who should know better than I,
bottled up as you and I have been, the two of us, together.
What is it now, near to a lifetime? Ah, the soul,

the soul! How in the end we worry about its disposition,
as if the body, too, wasn't just another name
for what you would, if you could, sell

separately on the cheap, down river. Admit it, though,
if wishes were fishes, . . . didn't I reel you in a boat load?
Yeah, and beware of what you wish for. I hear you.

Sorry about that. Look, the world as it has come to be
known, as they tell you it is, would make a nothing of us
both. Did you ever really believe that thing about being

every man for himself and the Devil take the hindmost?
Hindmost, foremost, how can it matter? It's all a splitting
of hairs. Something to amuse the kids.

As if you or I alone could take a yardstick to eternity
running for a touchdown the length of a football field.
And for old time's sake— you want to keep what?

the game ball? Are you still with me on this?
Do you follow me?
Can I be called in any way for interference?

43

Importunately

Imp (parenthetically speaking) is
a figment, meaning
just between you and me,

a body of want
out of a body of longing born,

that could not otherwise be,
between feces and urine—
the Devil and the Deep Blue Sea.

Imp Goes Fishing Anyway

Not that he has anything to fish with, or for.

Is it the water in the river
or the river's banks that flow
into which he does not step
twice (he seems to ask himself),
no stomach for the catch— if truth be told.
In the state he's in
how should he ever know?

On all that hungers,
on all that hunger grows,
if there weren't so many mouths to feed
(he seems to ask himself),
surely then he'd know
what all those teeth are for.

Poor soul, as if the life he wore
was but a pair of muddy shoes
slipped off as much as on again
and placed at someone's door.
Is it inside the house he wants
(he seems to ask himself),
Hello! Is any body there?

Who knocks and hears
but will not answer.
Who's there to say *Goodbye*
when no one's home.

Imp as Imponderable

Consider the Imp
that, everywhere, is I Am.
As if he had the ears to hear them by,
finger, nose, and eye,
ten thousand times times ten:
I am! I am! I am!

Was it the cry in the wilderness
out of the body's wordless rend—
star-flung, or did it leap
from the tower to the bridge?
Volition's insistent involuntary pushed?

The mother to be in ecstasy,
the infant's silent nursing at her breast.
The Ai! Ai! Ai! of . . . *Why*
have you forsaken me?
The Ecce Puer in
O, father, forgive your son.

49

Impetigo

Imp was beside himself.

His own thoughts made something of him,
surely (but what was that?), when bought
with the price of a doubt.

What ate at him, admittedly, was a niggling.
An itch he could never quite reach to scratch.

But what to do,
being an ineffable, an inkling,
a pale layer after layer
see-through onion skin,
his every outside same as within
clear through.

He'd rather wear a hair shirt.

If only he'd grow an abscess, a boil, a pox,
a show of efflorescent equanimity
in the face of his dis-ease.
Better to be a chancre dripping with pus.
Better to be a thing of substance
going to rot.

Was he overly tired? Unless? No. Not that.
Bored, was more like it, of looking
into the mirror that was everywhere himself,
but no one in particular.

He could be anybody. And was,
he reflected, suddenly inspired.

And, as if capable
of granting himself his own first wish,
came upon that smile which is,
as much as not, infectious.
And felt himself,
if somewhat falsely
feverish,

spreading.

An Imposition

Imp woke with a start.

No one was there—
no one ever was.

Still, he thought, or so he thought,
someone with him said,
Say you're from Missouri,
THE SHOW ME STATE
what comes to mind?

Imp looked as if
into a mirror,
wavered undecided,
coalesced

into an inkblot.

The usual Rorschach
was his guess.

Surely, it's the bird in hand,
the pudding in the mouth of proof,
if not the entire bush they want,
a snake that would have bit them
if it could.

And here the witness stood.
How about that picture worth
a thousand words?

Was it someone's other spoke?

By writ of habeas corpus
bring all before the court!

Imp felt himself falling
rock a bye baby in the tree tops.
Before less than none caught him up again
he thought, or so he thought:
it's not the bough breaking,
it's not the cradle rocked,
it's not a tree at all I'm in,
but a silent wind
blows through me knocks
the forest flat.

And what about London Bridge,
were you in on that caper too?

Innocent as much as guilty Sir,
or Ma'am, rather,
Imp heard himself say, confused.

Imp looked, as he looks now through
the wrong end of a telescope,
as night looks between the stars.
Was it the Hanging Judge he saw there,
the Queen of Hearts shouting,
"Off with his head!"
or— just you and me on trial here
before the sentence read?

Impending

Pyrophoric, flint struck against steel,
the star-spark plunge of the meteor
into excelsior's sweet night fern.
He might yet set the world on fire
just to see it burn.

But what was there left of him to sell?
Back-alley furtive that he was,
or thought he had become.   A shadow
haunter of cobbled streets, a rattler of locks
of shuttered midnight apothecary shops—
ointments sold there on the sly
as guard against the clap, the evil eye.
An estuary fog, the gangrenous green
surrounding Mercury's light
nailed there like a sign
above a house of ill-repute.

Perhaps he was a late Victorian after all.
Or, if Continental, a priapic Tea Pot Toulouse-Lautrec
but without the prodigy of a spout.

It's true, he preferred the oil lamp,
the flickering candle's glow
the warm and sooty air, the beery breath,
the love-talk secret and low.
The harlot camphors rising behind closed doors.
The shouts of ecstasy, or was it a cry of pain,
or the dog's lonely chained-up howl—

but how should he know the difference in the end?
The body lifeless. The body born again.

With no right of refusal,
no guarantee of return—
who would give him purchase now
for all the untold wishes he possessed?

Impecunious *(solvency insoluble)*

What was it moved him so:
over the dam and under a bridge

too far?

To and fro, to and fro—
an inch deep, a mile wide,
as much above as below?

(Could he be that Everywhere, but never
a drop to drink?)

Here a fish out of water at gasp for air.
There a Leviathan of abyssal calm,
with Jonah at home within.

(Had he ever, or had he, always, been?)

A question without answer, or the answer
staring back at him in every face.
Or was he merely Self absorbed?
A what was or is or meant to be
scratched in the sand by a childish hand
the moment the sea wrack rolls in.

The Imposture

Who are we, anyway to be so ill conceived?
I say it's you, you say it's me.
As if it were a secret vice to be a deceiver
indistinguishable from the one deceived.

about the artist

Over the past few years my focus has been to explore the intersection between intention and chance. Sometimes after making a series of random marks and passages I'm tempted to believe that I can exercise choice by rejecting some and retaining others. Sometimes I see images in the marks and believe I choose to develop them. Sometimes it seems I choose to prefer one painting or drawing over another.

Perhaps this is a pointless exploration though when you pause to think about it because even intention is mired in chance. At the very deepest inflection point between one choice and another it's nothing other than chance that flips the switch.

—DONALD GOLDER (2019)

To see more of Donald Golder's work: instagram.com Search for dwgolder.

about the author

ROBERT MURPHY's poems have appeared in the literary periodical *Smartish-Pace*, as well as the *Colorado Review, the Notre Dame Review, The Cultural Society, Marsh Hawk Review, Galatea Resurrects, Live Mag!, Prints into Poetry, Merle as Muse - Poetry Inspired by the Art of Merle Rosen*, and the Chicago based journal *LVNG*. He is the author of a chapbook *Not for You Alone*, (Dos Madres Press, 2004), *Life in the Ordovician - Selected Poems* (Dos Madres Press, 2007), and *From Behind the Blind* (Dos Madres Press, 2013).

He is a 2000 winner of the William Bronk Foundation prize for poetry.

Robert Murphy is also executive editor and publisher of Dos Madres Press. He is married to the iconographer and painter Elizabeth Hughes Murphy, who is both book designer and illustrator for Dos Madres Press.